DESIGNS ON FOLIAGE

Some seasonal sugarcraft ideas, with special emphasis upon the use of leaf shape, colour, growing habit, and other related subjects.

Margaret Ford

CelCakes

© Copyright Margaret Ford 1991.

Published by CelCakes, Gate Helmsley, York.

ISBN 1 872896 02 2

Photography by Chris Mason, York.

Artwork by Maxiprint.

Designed and printed by Maxiprint, Colour Printers, York.

CONTENTS

NTRODUCTION

Although I am very fond of making sugar flowers for display and cake decoration, the beauty and interest of leaves seems to be worthy of more attention. Rarely are flowers seen or produced without an abundance of foliage and throughout this booklet I hope to give leaves a new emphasis.

Wherever we live, and whatever the time of year, there is such a variety in leaf shape, colour and size. We surround ourselves with indoor plants, especially through the winter months, and they are a ready and accessible subject for attractive arrangements in sugar.

A predominance of leafy greens may not be within the sugarcraft brief or your natural choice, but I hope you will enjoy looking at, and trying out some new ideas — brightly coloured leaves, fruits, birds, and even fairies, give scope for something different. The occasional flower and/or ribbon should not be shunned, of course, and may be complementary to a design that is essentially "non-floral".

Explanatory notes are given for the cake decorations, as well as for some other sugarcraft techniques. The ideas are presented as a catalyst for your own thoughts and skills. I have been delighted by the response to "Designs on Wiring" and hope that now you will be encouraged to "turn over a new leaf".

Margaret Ford

ACKNOWLEDGEMENT

With thanks to my husband David, and daughters Louise (poems) and Sarah (harvest festival cake), for their help and support in producing this booklet.

3

NEW LEAVES

VEINERS AND VEINING

Although it is possible to purchase rubber and plastic veiners, it
very simple and inexpensive to make your own using latex liqui
If you follow the instructions below, you will be able to make
kinds of veiners, and by exchanging your moulds with frienc
you should very quickly build up an impressive collection.

STAGE 1

Collect some fresh leaves, making sure that they are goc
specimens (immature leaves that are not well veined, are n
suitable). You may want several sizes, but remember that th
scale of cake decorations is such that the smaller sizes w
probably be the most useful. Take some modelling clay c
compound (eg. Fymo), and roll out flat, but not too thinly (t
avoid the finished mould being fragile). Press the **back** of th
sample leaf into the clay and smooth over with your finger t
ensure a good impression. If you are using a leaf with ver
heavy veins (eg. primrose leaf) then it may be necessary t
reduce the stalk by trimming with scissors before pressing int
the modelling clay. This prevents the leaf being too coarsel
defined.

STAGE 2

From a long sausage shape of clay, carefully mould a low (abou
a quarter of an inch) wall round the edge of the leaf impression
making sure that it has a good seal to the base, and then bake th
"mould" in the oven, if required, according to the instruction
on the modelling clay packet. If the oven is too hot, the
modelling compound will be inclined to bubble and the moulc
will be unsatisfactory.

STAGE 3

When hardened, brush a very thin layer of liquid latex over the
bottom of the mould to cover the leaf impression completely
and then put in a warm place until dry (a thin layer of the latex
usually clears within about half an hour). Once the first layer
has cleared, carefully pour in more liquid latex until the mould
is almost full (thick veiners give more durable usage).

Dry out thoroughly in a warm atmosphere for several hours (overnight in an airing cupboard works well!). The latex veiner will only be ready when it has lost all the milky appearance and seems relatively transparent. Remove from the mould and dust with cornflower before use.

NOTE

If you regularly use a dried piece of corn-on-the-cob husk, take a fresh piece of husk and try making a latex veiner from it. You will find that it is more pliable and more durable. It is almost impossible to achieve a realistic veining on some leaves (eg. primrose) with a veining tool, and you will find your latex veiners invaluable.

MAKING LEAVES

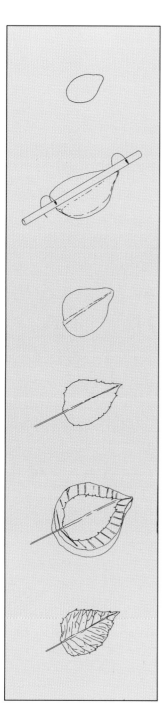

The following notes are intended as a general guide to making leaves (see page 51 for an explanation of pastes etc.):

STAGE 1

Colour some flower/petal paste light green (using gooseberry green or a similar colouring). Although the paste may seem to be pale in colour, this will be an advantage at the colouring stage, when it is easy to darken light paste, but more difficult to add lighter shades to a dark leaf. Form the paste into an elongated teardrop-shape and roll out sideways from the centre leaving a central ridge ready for the covered wire.

Using a leaf cutter or template, cut out the desired shape.

STAGE 2

Make a tiny tight hook on the end of a fine covered wire, dip into gum and insert into the ridge whilst holding the paste between thumb and forefinger – in this way, you will feel the bent wire move through the paste and can ensure that it does not protrude through the surface.

STAGE 3

Use a leaf veiner to obtain the appropriate markings on your leaf and then either in the palm of your hand, or on a firm foam pad, thin the leaf edges. Leave the leaf to dry, supporting if necessary to achieve a natural shape.

STAGE 4

When completely dry, dust with petal dusting powder (eg. moss green mixed with either brown, black or skintone gives a range of colours) both front and back, without making the colouring too even – leaves naturally have lighter and darker areas. Some leaves have pinkish tinges on the edges and occasionally pinkish blotches. This effect can be achieved by dusting the leaf edges with a flat brush dipped in a mixture of plum and black powder. Do not worry if some of the powder falls onto the leaf surface – some leaves naturally have coloured blotches, and so this can be an advantage.

Quickly pass the leaf through a jet of steam (from kettle spout) without getting it too wet. This will "fix" the colours and merge them together. The shiny appearance may gradually disappear, and if so, a more natural sheen can be obtained by softening a little white fat and brushing gently onto the surface of the leaf.

LEAF TEMPLATES

Although there are many leaf cutters available, sometimes it is necessary to work from cardboard templates. Simply trace round the outside edge of the leaf and transfer this to thin card or even thin plastic material (used food packaging etc.). When making veiners, it can be very useful to use the same leaves to make

cardboard templates, and then the leaf shape and veiner are identical in size.

SOME VARIEGATED LEAVES

SPIDER PLANT: Make the leaves by rolling out cream coloured paste and cut long narrow shapes. The leaves can be dried long and straight, curved into interesting arches, or looped into leafy bows by joining the leaf tip to the base. When dry, dust the outer edges with green powder to give the effect of a pale centre bounded by green. Groups of small leaves, taped firmly to the end of a long wire make an attractive spray extension and looks like the characteristic young plants.

IVY: Make the leaves from cream coloured petal paste and when dry, dust with green shades as described above. Alternatively, eye-catching ivy leaves can be made by making a leaf cutout in green paste and placing on top of it a slighly smaller cutout in either a lighter green or cream paste. It is important to get the two layers very thin, so that the finished leaves do not appear bulky. When colouring ivy, try adding touches of yellow powder to obtain a more realistic effect.

FOLIAGE SPRAYS

Leaves can be categorised by their size, shape, colour and growing habit (see charts on pages 44-45). Ivy leaves are ideal for a hanging or trailing aspect, the spider plant for arching extensions, whilst some ferns give contrast by their erect spikes amidst the softer rounded shapes of other leaves.

The use of tree leaves, buds and branches can add a new dimension to a display. The front cover of this booklet shows birch leaves and catkins, so naturally framing a springtime nesting place for two small birds. In similar fashion, autumnal moods are evoked by maple leaves tinted in reds, browns, yellow and gold.

There is a surprising range of colour in foliage − not only in different leaves, but also in the same leaf at different times of the year. Many house plants are multi coloured and sometimes blotched or speckled. All these combine to provide many interesting ways in which to introduce that special effect into your sugarcraft designs.

When you design a cake decoration based on leaves, the following elements need to be considered:

- the setting of the spray − its relationship and proportion to the cake and positioning...

- the overall size of the arrangement − whether it will be compact or open...

- the natural habit of the plants being represented − trailing, squat or very erect...

- the different shape of the leaves being used − and how they blend together...

- the different colours of the leaves − and how they complement or contrast with each other...

- the focal point of the arrangement − use of brightly coloured leaves, a flower, a bird, a branch...

8

It is important to consider the combined effect of leaves in a spray, and also the order in which the spray is assembled. Start with the outer framework, which determines the overall size and outline, and then gradually work towards the centre, so that prominence is given to leaves in the focal area. You may find it helpful to build up the spray in sub-sections, to be joined together later.

The **outer** zone includes those plants with trailing habit (eg. periwinkle) and thin spiked leaves (eg. spider plant) which give a leafy boundary and overall shape to the arrangement.

The **inner** zone includes those leaves which give some cover, but which also have an openness, giving the impression of space. Leaves with irregular edges or ones which are multi-lobed are very suitable (eg. chrysanthemum or fern leaves) because they add decoration and prevent the spray from looking too solid.

The **central** zone includes the main covering leaves which would normally be rounded or broad in shape. This gives body and stability to the spray and helps to disguise posy spikes, the securing ball of paste or the top of the supporting stand. This zone would also include the focal point (eg. Begonia Rex leaves). By using variegated leaves in the central area, a solid shape will appear far more open than it actually is and give a deceptive lightness to the spray. Similarly, moving the focal subject right out of the central area can have dramatic results (see wedding cake design).

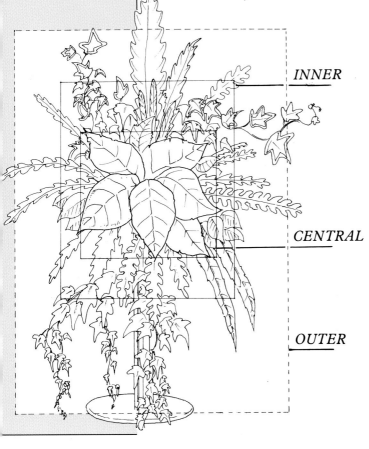

INNER

CENTRAL

OUTER

SPRING

SPRINGTIME

'Tis only in the springtime that the gambling lambs are seen,
When buds are bursting into life and leaves are fresh and
green.
The April showers come and go, whilst rainbows arch the sky,
And it's not long after hatching that young chicks begin to fly.

Pussy willow and birch catkins swaying gently in the breeze,
And promises of fruits to come is the blossom on the trees.
Whilst daffodils and crocus give some colour to the ground,
It's bird-song and the cuckoos note that fill the air with sound.

SOME SUGARCRAFT THEMES

Birds and bird nests...
moths and butterflies...
opening buds and new leaves...
twigs and catkins...
wild plants in the hedgerow...
lambs... eggs and chicks...
blossoms... maypole dancing...
scarecrow... rainbow and
shower clouds

WIGS AND ATKINS

One of the delights of springtime is to see delicate pollen laden hazel or birch catkins swinging in the breeze. Making catkins is not difficult, even though it may take a little time.

STAGE 1

Using a very small blossom plunger (a $^3/_{16}$ mini plunger is ideal) cut out several "blossoms" in cream coloured petal paste and before they have time to dry, quickly thread a needle and cotton through the paste cutouts.

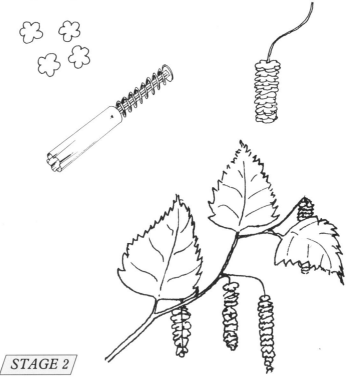

STAGE 2

When completely dry, colour with brown and yellow dusting powder and then attach to sprays — catkins can be displayed simply on bare twigs, with tiny green leaf buds, or as shown on the front cover, when the new birch leaves have developed.

11

TWIGS

To make twigs, bind several 24g wires together with bro
coloured florist's tape. Occasionally give a few extra turns of
tape to form a bump to resemble the budding points on
twig. At this point, tiny green pieces of paste, or tiny leaflet
opening buds on a fine wire, can be bound into place.

The dusting of the twigs is very important and the use
brown, green and grey tints may be needed to get a reali
finish. Because twigs have a little detail other than their sh
and colour, try to work from real examples if possible.

"PUSSY WILLOW" CATKINS

In a similar way to the making of the twigs described above,
is easy to include larger wired pieces of white paste to resem
willow catkins.

To give the effect of pollen, it is usually sufficient to moist
the white paste with gum and then dip into a mixture of whi
and yellow textured colouring (eg. sugartex or semolina mix
with powder colour).

Willow catkins can be a very pleasing addition to foliage spra
because they have a unique attraction of their own.

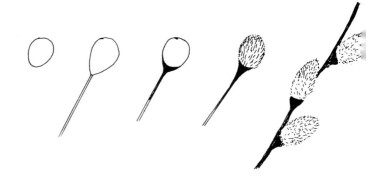

MAKING BIRDS

Foliage can be really enhanced by the addition of butterflies, ladybirds etc., but for a special effect, birds are an obvious choice. Though you may be cautious about bird modelling, the results can be very satisfying, and it is not as difficult as it might first appear. The most difficult parts of the bird to model are the wings and tail; because the paste dries so quickly there is little time for feather markings and shaping. Plastic wing and tail moulds do make the process much simpler.

HOW TO MAKE BIRDS

STAGE 1

Make the bird tail from white or cream coloured flower paste by pressing a fairly thin layer into one side of the tail mould. Using the locating buttons, snap into place the other half of the mould and then press together between fingers, so that the paste gets a good and detailed impression on each side. Carefully remove the paste, and trim the edges with scissors before shaping into a 'v' and drying. If a narrow tail is required the sides can be trimmed.

STAGE 2

Make the required body shape from a piece of paste moulded as shown (more bird shapes etc. are shown in the notes on page 48). It may be helpful to slightly hollow the body where open spread wings join. You will find that pictures in books and china ornaments are a really good guide to achieving a realistic body pose. The bird's head should be turned a little to the right or left and

sometimes a little up or down to create an attentive and "livin
stance. Before the body dries, attach a dried tail piece
making a slit and inserting it into the soft paste. Use paste g
(gum mixed with petal paste) to join the bird parts.

STAGE 3

Using the moulds as already described, make the wings. T
open wings should be dried over a curved surface. For the sm
wings, it may be necessary to fill behind with a small sausag
shaped piece of paste to get a fuller shape (as for the small squ
bird on the front cover). For a bird with wings tightly clos
(eg. the robin), fix the small wing pieces into place whilst st
soft, so that they blend closely to the dried body shape.

STAGE 4

When the bird body and the wings have dried, assemble th
bird using paste glue, and then paint as desired, using pictur
as a guide. After painting, scratching the paste surface with
craft knife can enhance the feathered effect required. Finally,
light dusting will help to cover any excessive scratches. Th
completed bird can be set on a piece of roughened paste (se
page 35 on details for making rough log). Carefully pipe th
bird legs and feet in brown/grey icing before adding to the cak
setting.

14

Make a bird's nest by hollowing a piece of brown paste into a small bowl shape and leave to dry. This can then be covered

by entwined twigs, made either with royal icing (fine writing tube) or by pushing softened paste through a clay gun fitted with a fine mesh disc. When dry, dust with different brown and grey tints and decorate with "moss" (easily made with the clay gun), or by pushing softened paste through a metal sieve.

A PASTURE PLATE

Some of the delicate meadowland plants are difficult
assemble into a cake display, and yet they can be very attracti
for a pastillage plate decoration (presented at the side of a cak
and also as a gift).

To make the plate, colour some pastillage with light green pas
colouring and roll out until larger than the plate you wish to u
as the mould – it is best to select a plate that has no sharp edge
rims or dimples. Invert the plate onto the rolled paste and c
round. Transfer the circle of paste onto the plate (dusted wi
cornflower) and leave to dry out. When dried, the edge may l
finished by piping a beading in royal icing.

THE PLANTS

I have selected some of the more unusual wild plants for th
plate featured here, and the following notes give details on ho
they can be made . . .

VETCH: For the vetch leaves, thin the paste as normal, inse
a hooked wire and cut out a small pointed leaf shape, with
single vein down the centre. The tiny pink flowers are made b
flattening a very small ball of pink paste onto the end of
hooked wire, then placing in the centre of a mini rose petal, an
folding round. A second petal can be added for the more matur
flower. The tendrils are made by twisting the end of the mai
wire round the handle of an artist's brush or tiny modellin
stick.

PLANTAIN: The plantain is made by placing a ball of gree
paste on the end of a hooked wire and shaping it into a tapere
oval. After inserting a ring of short, bent white stamens, th
head needs to be dried before dusting with brown and gree
shades of powder colour. The broad dark leaves are cut wit
scissors and dusted with dark green colouring. They offer goo
cover for the centre of the arrangement and make an importan
contrast to some of the other green shades.

CLOVER: The flower heads look complicated, but are easy t
make by taking a ball of green paste and fixing to the end of
covered wire. This should then be covered completely with
thin layer of either white or pink paste, depending upon the
colour of the clover being made.

16

Using a pair of fine scissors, the ball of paste is very finely snipped round the base and then progressively to the top, so as to resemble the clover head. If clipped correctly, the green paste will show at the base of each snip just as seen in the real plant.

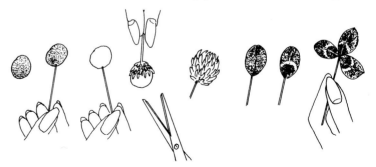

The clover leaves are made using tiny rose petal cutters and light green paste. When the paste has dried, the white markings are painted on with white colouring mixed with alcohol.

Finally the complete leaves are dusted with green petal powder, so that the decorative markings show through, and assembled in groups of three (and occasionally four!).

SUMMER

INTO SUMMER

The summer days are long and warm, with sunshine beating down,
They ripen all the fruits and turn our cornfields golden brown.
The hedgerows now are brimmed with life - insects on the wing,
And bees reap the full advantage of the nectar flowers bring.

It's the time of year for cricket or for tennis in the shade,
And early evening barbecues, as the heat begins to fade.
For picnics on the riverbank, whilst graceful swans glide by,
Surrounded by boats and butterflies, beneath a cloudless sky.

SOME THEMES FOR SUGARCRAFT

Flying kites (many exciting shapes and colours)...
fountains, waterfalls, garden ponds and water lilies...
bees and butterflies...
swallows, finches and other birds... rabbits, hedgehogs...
pony trekking and camping...
heather moors...
the spreading chestnut tree and woodland... garden parties and fetes...
cornfields and meadows...
fresh fruits... summer gardens and shows...
weddings... summer holidays at the seaside... the river and boating...hedgerow scenes

The following more detailed notes continue the wild plant theme:

SHEPHERD'S PURSE

STAGE 1

The flower head is made by winding green cotton thread round a finger several times and then placing a fine covered wire through the loop and twisting it tightly. Bind with florist's tape before cutting open the loops. Trim the threads to an appropriate length with scissors. The effect of the flower heads is achieved by moistening the cotton tips with gum and then dipping them in white textured colouring.

STAGE 2

The heart-shaped seed pods are made by using a very small wild rose cutter (or mini heart-shaped plunger) and inserting a fine wire at the base of the heart. They are left to dry, before dusting with powder colouring. Finally the pods and flower heads are assembled as shown.

HEMLOCK

In a very similar way, it is possible to make very attractive hemlock...

STAGE 1

Using very fine covered wires, make up several flower heads in exactly the same manner as described above, but with some more full than others - the hemlock head has some larger fuller florets, surrounded by smaller ones to the outer edges.

STAGE 2

Dip the individual moistened heads into textured colouring and then assemble the main hemlock head by taping several of the finished flower heads together. Open out into the appropriate size and shape.

STAGE 3

When assembled, some of the flower heads re-dipped into t
colouring will give a fuller effect. The hemlock leaves are ve
'feathery' and difficult to make without cutters - a Jem dai
cutter however, can be used as a suitable substitute.

BULLRUSHES

Bullrushes are quickly made in sugar, and yet they add
sophistication to the "watery" setting of ducks or swans on
cake. They are particularly effective placed at the side of a cak
when tall enough to stand proud of the top, and in clumps
different heights.

STAGE 1

The rushes are made by colouring some paste brown an
threading a sausage shape onto the end of a moistened covere
wire. The paste should be pushed on until the end of the wi
protrudes. After drying, the paste can be dusted with dar
brown petal powder.

STAGE 2

The long narrow leaves should be hand-cut from light gree
paste and left to dry in different bent and curving shapes. Afte
dusting the leaves, the finished bullrushes can be assembled.

SUMMER WEDDING

Even with all the excitement of summer, there is nothing like a wedding. Some of the ideas on these pages may seem a little "different", but I hope that they might encourage you to move away from the more traditional settings. The simplicity and gracefulness of the peace lily makes it an ideal choice for adding a special touch to a foliage design and by lifting the focal point beyond the spray outline, the result can be very striking.

PEACE LILIES FOR A WEDDING CAKE

STAGE 1

Place a small sausage of white paste on the end of two fairly lo__
24g wires, taped together. Leave to dry for a while and th__
moisten the surface with gum and attach tiny beads of wh__
paste until completely covered. Allow to dry.

STAGE 2

Cut out the petal shape (see diagram) of the main part of t__
flower in white paste and attach to a 28g wire. After shapin__
and whilst soft, attach to the flower centre allowing the pe__
edges at the bottom to wrap round and join. Tape togeth__
before leaving to dry.

STAGE 3

Colouring is done using different shades and amounts of gre__
paste or powder colour mixed with water. The flower needs__
very delicate pale green "wash" before the prominent gre__
veins are painted into place. The leaves can be hand-cut in lig__
green paste and darkened with dark green (eg moss green mix__
with black) powder colouring.

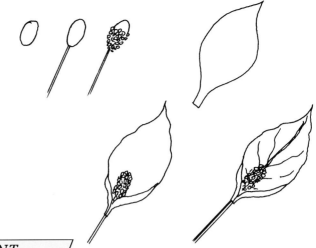

The piggyback plant is quite a novelty with its smaller leaves growing out of the top of larger ones, but it also gives scope for different colour effects, having so many shades of green with several speckled variations.

STAGE 1

Hand cut the leaf shapes (or use templates) in many different sizes from light green paste, and after thinning, put them onto hooked wires (the very tiny leaves should be put onto 30g or 33g wires and the larger ones on 28g wires). Allow to dry thoroughly.

STAGE 2

Dust on the darker green areas, and "spot" or speckle by tapping a brush, which has been dipped in powder colouring, over the leaf surface. When all the colouring has been added, pass through a jet of steam to blend and "fix". Assemble the leaf combinations and use to decorate sprays.

(For details on the pink polka dot leaves, see page 43)

23

THE WATER GARDEN

WATER LILIES

The water lily has been selected here, more because of its leav[es]
than the flower. The single flower in the arrangement is real[ly]
enhanced by the natural habit of the plant - the new leav[es]
furled and held high and the buds below and bent upward[.]
The open leaves are held in a level plain, as if floating upon t[he]
water surface.

STAGE 1

The lily leaves are cut by using different sized round objects [as]
a template and then cutting out a "v" segment, before wirin[g.]
The radial veining can be done with a veiner tool, and som[e]
leaves are curled towards the centre. When dry, the leav[es]
should be dusted with different green shaded powder mixtur[es]
(made from different greens and blacks), and the furled leav[es]
should be finished with pinkish tints.

STAGE 2

The broad buds are moulded from a ball of white paste place[d]
on the end of a hooked wire. It is then entirely covered with [a]
thin layer of brown paste. After lightly cutting across the to[p]
with a craft knife, the four brown sepals can be slightly peele[d]
back to reveal the flower buds. Cuts in the white paste can b[e]
opened to give the effect of the flower beginning to open.

STAGE 3

The inner flower centre is made using yellow cotton threa[d]
wound round a finger 20-30 times, and wired (as in shepherd'[s]
purse) before being dipped into yellow textured colouring. Th[e]
outer part of the centre is made up from several stamens tha[t]
have had paste rolled round them to make them thicker. The[y]
are then coloured yellow and when dried, taped around th[e]
cotton centre.

The petals are hand cut (see diagram for shapes) from white paste. Assemble the first petal layer (6 smallest petals) around the centre using paste glue and allow to dry. Similarly use paste glue to assemble the next layer using 4 larger petals, and after drying, the third layer with 6 petals of the next size. Finally add an outer layer of 8 petals. (An additional outer layer of four greenish sepals may be added).

/ SWANS /

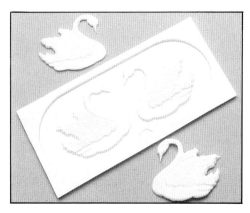

The swans on the cake below were made using flat relief moulds with a mixture of petal paste and sugarpaste (alternatively use sugarpaste mixed with gum traga-canth). Roll out the paste and press into the mould, trimming away round the edges with a fine palette knife. When lifted from the mould, the swans can be dried flat or curved, depending upon the type of cake side being decorated. They can also be assembled together on the top of a cake by fixing two at a slight angle to each other, decorated with leaves or flowers (or on the side of a valentine cake, they could be positioned looking at each other with a heart cutout in the middle.)

AUTUMN

AUTUMN

It's harvest time once again, and combines reap the corn,
And early in the mornings the first dews and mists are born.
Slowly the leaves start to turn and flutter to the ground,
Ripe brambles are for picking and fresh mushrooms can be found.

Lanterns are cut for hallowe'en, whilst children "trick or treat",
Standing round the bonfire, hot potatoes are good to eat!
Spider's webs glint in the frost, as the air gets sharp and cold,
Squirrels and badgers think of sleep - the well-known habit of old.

SUGARCRAFT IDEAS AND SUGGESTIONS

Harvest festival celebrations... traditional corn dolly decoration
Toadstools and mushrooms... Snails and scurrying insects.
blackbirds and thrushes
looking for berries...
frosted foliage...
spider's webs...
indoor plant decor...
mysteries of hallowe'en...
foliage fairies...
fruit and nuts...
vegetables etc.

FRUIT AND FUNGI

BRAMBLES

There is no better loved wild fruit than the blackberry or bramble, and it looks delightful in sugar:

STAGE 1

Make leaves in the usual way from light green paste, using the rose leaf cutters, and they should be fairly heavily veined. When dry, dust with moss green and skintone colouring to resemble the autumn tints. Fix the colours with a jet of steam.

STAGE 2

To make the fruits, place a ball of paste on the end of a hooked wire and taper slightly towards a rounded cone. When **partly dry,** moisten with gum and attach tiny beads of paste from the base upwards - the fruits can be green, pinkish, red or purple according to how ripe the fruit should appear. When completely dry, add a small calyx and give the berries a gloss, using confectioner's glaze.

STAGE 3

Make the flower centres from cotton thread fixed to a wire (see previous methods) and add a small green calyx. Some of the "dead heads" will have no petals at all, but petals can be cut with a mini rose petal cutter, and carefully attached to the dry calyx. When completely dry the petal edges should be tinted with pink.

Hazel nuts can be very decorative because of their green "ru
and when the nuts begin to turn brown they give a pleasi
autumnal emphasis to even a very simple design.

STAGE 1

Take a small ball of paste and mould into a nut shape and ins
a hooked wire. From a jagged strip of green paste that has be
frilled on one side, curl round the nut, moistened with gum,
make the sheath. Allow to dry. The nuts can be coloured lig
green, through to shades of the characteristic hazel colour a
they should be assembled in clusters of two or three.

STAGE 2

The hazel leaves tend to have more yellow and brown tints
them than definite red and bronze shades, but when assembl
with the nuts, they are very distinctive.

MUSHROOMS AND TOADSTOOLS

Toadstools can be moulded as follows:

STAGE 1

Make the toadstool top from a thick disc in white or crean
paste. Mark the underside with a veining tool, by radiating ou
from the centre. Make an indentation in the centre where th
stalk will join. Allow to partly dry whilst making the stalk.

STAGE 2

For the stalk, roll a thin sausage shape and, after it has dried
little, moisten the end and press into place on the flat disc, s
that the top of the toadstool is pushed up slightly to give the
required shape. (By leaving the parts to dry a little before
assembly, a characteristic wrinkling will be seen on the paste
surfaces - leaving too long will result in cracking of course!)

STAGE 3

Colour with the desired dusting powder and set two or three
toadstools into a piece of paste as a base - a simple mossy bank
base can be made from a lump of paste where the surface has
been stippled with an old piping nozzle.

FOLIAGE FAIRIES

As an alternative to flowers and birds, a really attractive addition to a foliage design can be a small fairy, dressed in appropriate leaves and sepals. The fairy body can be made in a mould, or by hand modelling.

STAGE 1

A little planning makes the modelling task much easier, so decide on how the fairy will be positioned (sitting, standing, crouched etc) and look carefully at the limb shapes on page 50, or at pictures of fairies, to select the most suitable shapes for the arms and legs.

STAGE 2

From a ball of paste, mould into tiny sausage shapes, indenting for knees, ankles, elbows and wrists, using both fingers and a

modelling stick, as appropriate. Carefully shape at the ends,
feet and hands, and cut tiny fingers etc with fine scisso
Similarly model the body and head shapes, and allow all t
parts to dry before assembly. Attach with paste glue.

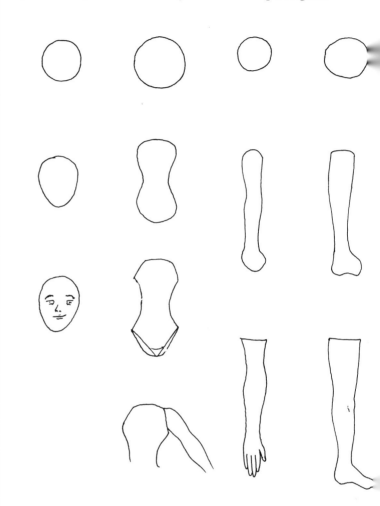

STAGE 3

Leaves, and parts of fruits or nuts should be used for the items
of clothing (eg a beech leaf tunic on the little boy on the back
cover and a bramble fruit and leaf dress on the bramble fairy).
Since it is difficult to make very fine hair in icing, it can be
useful to decide upon a suitable subject for a hat.

STAGE 4

The wing shapes can be varied, (several butterfly-type or
dragonfly-type shapes are very suitable), and they do not always
need to be fully opened. Cut paste to shape and roll very thinly
indeed. When dry, paint with a suitable colour tint and finish
with some silver snowflake to add a translucent effect.

For autumn beech leaves (as used for fairy on back cover), make leaves in the usual way in light green paste (use a template for the shape). When dry, dust with powder colours, starting with the palest colour first - yellow, then green and finally the bronze shades (made from skintone, brown and black mixtures).

For beech nuts, roll a ball of brown paste into a cone, hollow out and cut to four points. Roughen the outside by snipping with scissors.

31

HARVEST FESTIVAL

Making vegetables and fruit for a harvest festival cake can fun, and they are very easy to mould from marzipan...

CARROTS

Carrots should be moulded from a bright orange ball marzipan rolled into a pointed sausage shape. Indentations markings are made with a tiny modelling stick. The small lea top is made from a strip of marzipan that has been cut in strands at one end and then curled before fixing into place the end of the carrot.

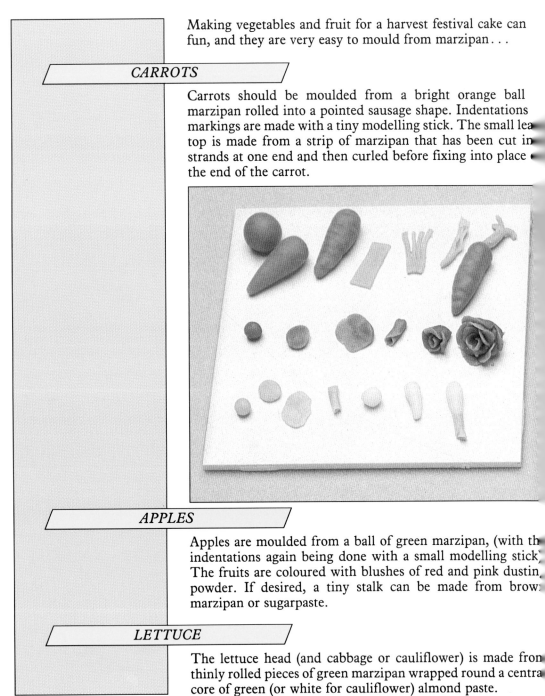

APPLES

Apples are moulded from a ball of green marzipan, (with th indentations again being done with a small modelling stick The fruits are coloured with blushes of red and pink dustin, powder. If desired, a tiny stalk can be made from brow: marzipan or sugarpaste.

LETTUCE

The lettuce head (and cabbage or cauliflower) is made from thinly rolled pieces of green marzipan wrapped round a centra core of green (or white for cauliflower) almond paste.

LEEKS

Leeks (and spring onions if done very fine) are made from white and light green coloured marzipan. The trimmed green top is made from a flattened piece of paste, rolled up, whilst the white bottom is moulded from a ball of white paste rolled into a half sausage before the two are merged together.

CORN

STAGE 1

To make corn, small beads of cream petal paste should be rolled onto the middle of white stamen cottons, so that the stamen end at the top resembles the husk. The grain should be veined and allowed to dry.

STAGE 2

Assemble the ears of corn by taping several grains together with white florist's tape before dusting with a mixture of brown and cream dusting powder.

WINTER

IN WINTER

The signs of winter are easy to see - the fog, the ice, the snow,
And the branches on the trees are bared in the biting winds that blow.
But there are cones on green pine trees and the holly berries, red
And at many a festive party, the mistletoe hangs over our head.

As the snowflakes flutter down to earth, the air is quiet and still,
And the hungry robin can be seen taking breadcrumbs from the sill.
Animals leave their footprints as they hunt in the frost and the cold,
As for those by the fire, they patiently wait for another year to
unfold.

THEMES FOR SUGARCRAFT

The many indoor plant varieties... dead leaves and twigs with
insects... skating and
skiing... christmas
foliage sprays...
frosted leaves...
icicles and snow
scenes... pheasant
in the snow...
snowflake designs...
robin and other birds
at a bird table...
stones and bark
with moss...
valentine cake...
snowdrops pushing
through dead leaves...
flower pot scene with
small animal etc...
silhouette branches
against the moon

TONES, BARK AND MOSS

Small stones and pebbles can be made from brown and grey pieces of paste, though some pleasing effects are also achieved by marbling different colours. To make larger rough stones and boulders:

STAGE 1

To make a rugged finish, or a rustic finish to pieces of bark, the paste should be moulded into the approximate shape needed, and then should be left until the outer surface has started to dry.

STAGE 2

Once slightly crusted, the paste needs to be reshaped a little so that it cracks and dimples without breaking up into small pieces. When satisfied with the effect, allow to dry completely.

STAGE 3

Colour with brown and greyish tints and add blotches of green. For bark, ridge the paste before the crusting stage, and then reshape before drying completely.

STAGE 4

To represent moss and lichen, small pieces of green or cream paste moistened with gum, can be smeared into place. Alternatively the moss can be "piped" from a clay gun. A final dusting will give the finished stone a realistic appearance (see page 29).

MAKING A PLANT POT

As a mould for a plant pot, the smaller sizes of plastic plant pots, available from a garden centre, are ideal and cost only a few pence (you may need to file off some ridges on the inside).

Colour petal paste with chestnut brown mixed with black paste colour to obtain the required shade and then mould to the inside of the plant pot. Take care not to get the paste too thin, and when dry, you will be surprised at how closely your sugar model resembles the traditional clay pot.

For a simple cake decoration, that also doubles as a gift, m: a small pot and put in it a colourful sugar plant to stand by t cake. The begonia is a very suitable choice, because it has su varied shape, finish and colour, making it very versatile for t non-floral decoration (obviously good for some floral dec ations as well). Another advantage to making displays fr

indoor plants is that it is very easy to obtain the real leaves copy over an extended period of time - something which alwa produces the best result!

STAGE 1

Using either a begonia leaf cutter or cutting out with cardboard template, make a leaf shape from pale green past vein, thin and frill the edges as preferred. Some begonias ha jagged edges, and this can be achieved by veining across th edge of the leaf on a firm foam pad.

STAGE 2

Make leaves of different sizes and also make leaves of differer orientation - some to the left and some to the right. A balance and natural display will need a mixture of both. Allow th leaves to dry thoroughly.

STAGE 3

Colour with dusting powder according to the leaf bein prepared. The begonia rex colourings should be copied from real leaves, or from illustrations, by dusting the specific area with the different colours.

CHRISTMAS DECORATIONS

Since there are many well-known methods for making holly, one is not repeated here. Instead, the following notes should give some ideas on how the traditional theme might be varied:

VARIATIONS ON THE HOLLY THEME

Holly made from sugar can be used very effectively either as decoration for the Christmas cake, or for novel table decoration. Try making some holly with light green leaves which are edged in pink, before being frosted with silver snowflake colouring. For the final touch, add white berries. Alternatively, the traditional dark green holly and bright red berries can be given a real heavy frost look by moistening the leaves, stems and berries with gum and then sprinkling thoroughly with very fine castor sugar granules. This can be extremely striking and can be used with other leaves as well — try it on some brambles for that early frost effect. The frosted effect is also very attractive on ivy and other berries — eg. a group of snowdrops near a plant pot with frosted ivy etc.

CONES AND DEAD LEAVES

Fir cones can be made simply by snipping a ball of brown paste which has been put onto a covered wire, in a similar way to the method for making the clover heads. Another method for cones starts with a cone of brown paste fixed to a covered wire and left to dry thoroughly. Miniature brown rose petals can be added starting at the top and working downwards. The petal edges are then opened up with a modelling stick.

Dead leaves are made in the usual way, but using a light brown paste. They should not be placed on wires, but veining does add to the authenticity. They should then be dried in twisted and slightly crumpled shapes, before being dusted with darker shades.

THE ROBIN

The robin, a favourite for Christmas decorations, is made in the same way as the other birds already described. Depending upon the particular setting, a preferred body shape should be selected from the body outlines shown on page 48.

STAGE 1

If the bird is to be sitting alert (as pictured in front of the plant pot) then it is important to make and dry the body (tail already in place) before adding the small wings. The wings are positioned whilst still soft so that they can be moulded to the shape of the bird and then be left to dry.

STAGE 2

For colouring, mix dark brown and black for the feathers, scratching with a craft knife to increase the feathery effect. The "red" breast should be coloured using skintone powder colour, mixed with a little orange. It is important that the model birds have a sharp glazed eye — colour carefully with black and touch with confectioner's glaze.

A NEW BABY

This bas relief design can be used either with a baby head for christening cake top, with a mouse head as an animal plaque, as a decoration for a child's birthday cake — all using the sam bed setting.

STAGE 1

For the baby's head, either model by hand or more convenient use a suitable baby head mould, and allow to dry befor colouring. The mouse head should be modelled from brow paste with fur markings being added with a veiner tool.

STAGE 2

As shown in the diagram, a wedge of paste with a hollow in (the pillow) and a larger hump of paste (the shaper for the quil should be fixed to the plaque.

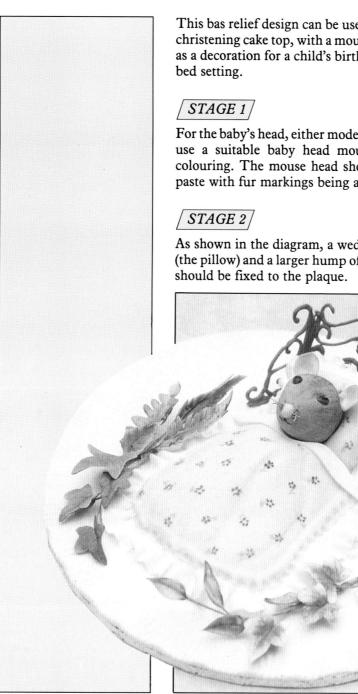

STAGE 3

Fix the head into position and roll out some white paste and cut a suitable rounded shape to make a throwover quilt. Add narrow frilled edges to the pillow and the quilt.

STAGE 4

Decorate the quilt by painting in tiny dot flowers all over to give the effect of a fabric design. Alternatively, pipe on a pattern with a very fine piping tube.

STAGE 5

Make a sugar bedhead by piping a scrolled design on butcher's wrap (acetate paper). When dried thoroughly, assemble around the pillow.

STAGE 6

Make a selection of leaves and decorate round the bed to complete the setting. A final touch can be to add one or two ladybird "attendants".

THROUGHOUT THE YEAR

INDOOR PLANTS

Indoor plants can offer an impressive range of colours for c
decoration...

SPECKLED LEAVES

To make the green leaves with white spots, make up the leave
in green paste in the usual way and dry thoroughly. With a ver
fine paintbrush, paint random white blotches on the lea
surface using white powder colour (or opaque white) mixec
with alcohol or rejuvenator spirit. When dry, dust the entire
leaf with a mixture of green (eg. moss green) and black, finally
passing it through steam to fix the colours.

PINK HYPOESTES

Pink hypoestes leaves (as used on the wedding cake) are made up in white paste (natural leaves are white on the underside) and when dry, are dusted on the top surface with pink powder colour. The green blotches and edges are then carefully painted on with a fine brush as described above.

FERN LEAVES

The following notes relate to making fern leaves using the "three-in-one fern cutter":

The principle, when using this cutter, is to select the particular leaf form — a common fern, a castor oil plant type or a house fern type — and then use the cutting edge of the cutter. After rolling out the paste, and before inserting the wire, first cut one side of the leaf, then turn the cutter over to cut the other side. You will find it very easy to make leaves of different sizes, just by cutting at a different angle across the paste.

When making the house fern, for example, you will need leaves of different sizes. After frilling the edges and colouring with darker dusting powder, to give the characteristic semi-variegated appearance, the leaves should be assembled into groups of three or five. The ferns make a very attractive and unusual addition to your foliage spray.

FOLIAGE COLOUR CHART

	LIGHT GREEN	DARK GREEN	VARIEGATED	WHITE/CREAM	YELLOW	PINK/RED	BROWN	MULTI-COLOUR	SPECKLED	PATTERNED	CATKINS/FRUIT/NUTS
BIRCH	●				●		●				●
BEECH	●	●			●	●	●				●
CHERRY	●	●			●	●					●
MAPLE	●	●	●	●	●	●	●		●		
BEGONIA	●	●	●	●	●	●	●	●	●	●	
POLKA DOT PLANT (Hypoestes)	●			●		●			●		
MARANTA	●	●		●			●			●	
POINSETTIA		●				●					
COLEUS	●	●	●	●	●	●	●	●	●	●	
CROTON (Codiaeum)		●			●	●			●		
PIGGYBACK PLANT (Tolmiea)	●	●			●					●	
HOUSE FERNS	●		●	●	●						
SPIDER PLANT	●		●	●	●						
IVY	●	●	●	●	●					●	
TRADESCANTIA	●	●	●	●		●					

FOLIAGE SHAPE AND HABIT

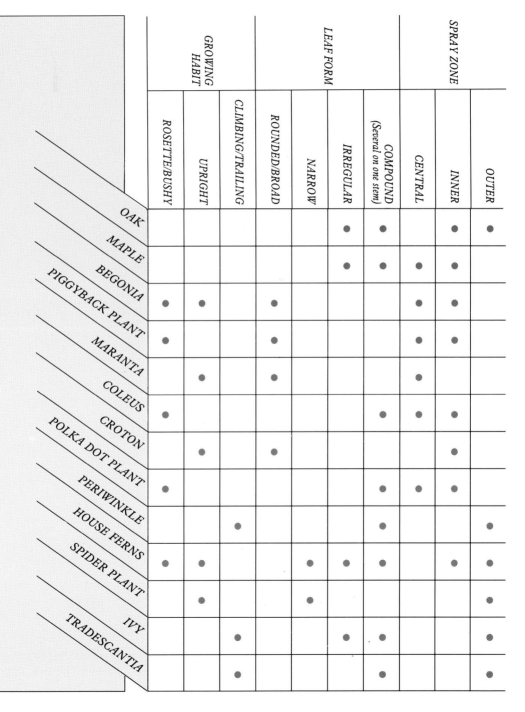

	GROWING HABIT			LEAF FORM				SPRAY ZONE		
	ROSETTE/BUSHY	UPRIGHT	CLIMBING/TRAILING	ROUNDED/BROAD	NARROW	IRREGULAR	COMPOUND (Several on one stem)	CENTRAL	INNER	OUTER
OAK						●	●		●	●
MAPLE						●	●	●	●	
BEGONIA	●	●		●				●	●	
PIGGYBACK PLANT	●			●				●	●	
MARANTA		●		●				●		
COLEUS	●						●	●	●	
CROTON		●		●					●	
POLKA DOT PLANT	●						●	●	●	
PERIWINKLE			●				●			●
HOUSE FERNS	●	●			●	●	●		●	●
SPIDER PLANT		●			●					●
IVY			●			●	●			●
TRADESCANTIA		●					●			●

SOMETHING DIFFERENT

Although foliage arrangements are usually green based, a[nd] coloured leaves are often limited to reds, yellows and brow[n] there is no reason why the natural colours should be faithful[ly] copied. When creating your foliage design, develop it aroun[d] colour scheme of your choice, not necessarily using natu[ral] colourings. You could try mixing a range of different brow[ns] and creams with turquoise and burgundy or, as in the examp[le] here black, white, grey, pink and dusky red . . .

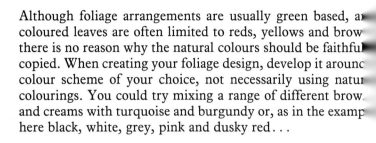

MAKING HONESTY

The white seed pods are made from two layers of very thi[n] white paste, where six tiny beads of pastes ("seeds") have bee[n] positioned on one layer before they are gummed together wit[h] a fine white covered wire between - the upper part of the wir[e] should be left protruding slightly. When dry, the honest[y] should be coloured with silver snowflake powder and steame[d] to give a translucent effect. Assemble into small sprays for us[e] later.

CATKINS

The catkins for this arrangement are made as already describe[d] (see page 12), though the stems are taped with black florist'[s] tape to give a striking contrast.

LEAVES

The leaves are hand cut from a pale grey petal paste (coloured by adding black) and after drying in various shapes are dusted with darker grey colouring, using a mixture of black and white dusting powder. The tips are coloured in pale pink.

THE ORCHIDS

The orchid-type flowers are cut freehand, though they could have been made using cutters. The colour of the darkest flower is mixed from mulberry, black and brown paste colouring. For the progressively lighter shades add increasing amounts of white petal paste. The back petals are made in dark grey petal paste. When dry, the edges of the pink petals can be dusted with grey powder (a simple mixture of black and white).

THE CAKE

The grey cake colouring is achieved by carefully adding a very small amount of black paste colouring to white sugarpaste - take care not to add too quickly and make the paste too dark.

BIRD SHAPES AND MOULDS

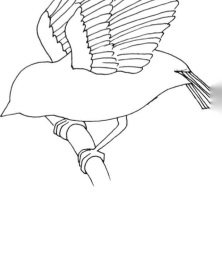

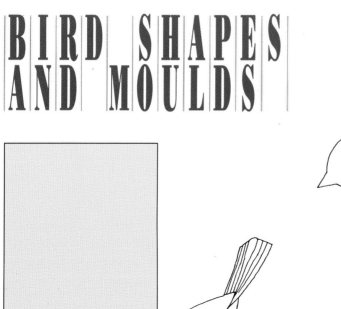

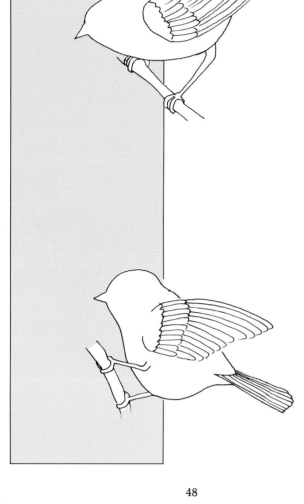

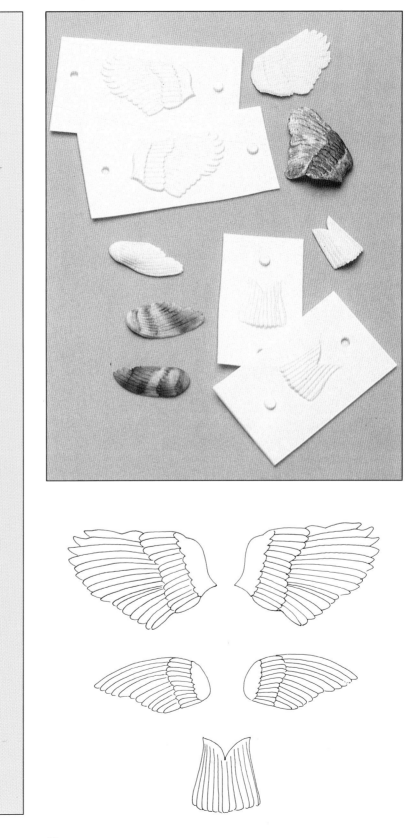

FAIRY SHAPES

LEGS

ARMS

WINGS

GUM - the term "gum" refers to either egg white (albumen), gum arabic solution or softened sugarpaste, and the particular usage will be determined by your own preference and experience.

PASTE GLUE - a mixture of petal paste and gum, worked with a tiny spatula until very soft and sticky. Paste glue is very useful for making strong joins and is ideal for attaching bird wings and fairy limbs. It is also ideal for repairing accidental breakages to dried leaves and flowers, because the repair is almost invisible if a paste colour the same as the leaf or petal is used.

PETAL PASTE - there are many recipes for petal paste (sometimes called flower paste) to be found in sugarcraft books. The one that I prefer, is the recipe often referred to as the "South African Recipe" and is made using a heavy duty mixer (eg Kenwood).

SUGARPASTE - sometimes called covering paste.

When making **birds,** the body should be made from a mixture of petal paste and sugarpaste, whilst the tail and wings should be made from petal paste. The nest is also made from a petal and sugarpaste mixture. For making **fairies,** the body and limbs should be made from a mixture of petal paste and sugarpaste, and petal paste is ideal for the wings which need to be very fine.

PRODUCT DETAILS

The following products should be available from your sugarcraft supplier:

Liquid latex - ask for "Veiner Maker"

Double-sided veiners - ask for "Great Impressions" moulds

Bird wing moulds, swan moulds etc. - ask for CelShapes moulds

Fern Cutter - ask for "Three-in-One Fern Cutter"

Modelling compound - Fymo can be obtained from craft shops and some stationers

Margaret Ford has been teaching sugarcraft techniques
several years both at local authority evening classes and fr
her own classroom near York. She regularly demonstrates
British Sugarcraft branch meetings, exhibitions and on
sugarcraft roadshows.

Margaret is increasingly making an impact at home a
overseas through her flair for innovative sugarcraft aids a
ideas. She has produced several booklets on making flowers a
wiring sprays and *Designs on Foliage* represents a natu
development into cake decoration based on other subjects.